THE WONDERFUL WORLD OF WORDS

19

King Noun and Queen Verb Agree

Dr Lubna Alsagoff

PhD (Stanford)

mc Marshall Cavendish
Children

Queen Verb and King Noun went for a walk.

They began to play their favourite game.

These tree grow well in our garden.

These tree grow well in our garden.

2

3

4

7

Choose the right word for each of the blanks.

soldier

soldier

The [_____] train hard every day.

The [_____] train hard every day.

anteater

anteater

An [_____] eat as many as a thousand ants a day.

[_____] eat as many as a thousand ants a day.

teacher

teacher

My [_____] love to sing.

All my [_____] love to sing.

8

(swim) (swim**s**)

Frog**s** [＿＿＿＿] very well.

(hop) (hop**s**)

The little frog [＿＿＿＿]
very quickly!

(climb) (climb**s**)

The lizard**s** [＿＿＿＿] up
the tree.

(look) (look**s**)

That lizard [＿＿＿＿] lost.

(love) (love**s**)

These boy**s** [＿＿＿＿]
to play football.

(kick) (kick**s**)

The boy usually [＿＿＿＿]
the ball with his left foot.

Cappy the Caterpillar wanted to play as well.
He decided to add conjunctions to the game.

Peter and Fran love ice cream.
Yes, indeed! They love ice cream.
Who loves ice cream more?
Fran loves ice cream but Peter loves ice cream much more than Fran!

The king and queen were deciding on which instruments to add to the WOW band.

The banjo sound🐝 wonderful.

The guitar sound🐝 wonderful too.

When or is used, look at the noun that is closest to the verb!

The banjo or the guitar sound🐝 like a wonderful instrument for our band.

Yes, banjo🐝 or guitar🐝 sound wonderful with the piano.

Shall we also add some trumpets?
What about a trombone?
Three trumpets or a trombone sound wonderful!
But we must choose. We can only have either the trumpets or the trombone.
The trombone or the trumpets sound equally good.

The king and queen could not decide which instrument to choose for their band. So they included all of them!

Put  in the boxes where it is needed.

Either the green cough syrup or the big white pill☙ taste ☐ the worst.

My sister or my brother☙ cheer ☐ me up with lovely treats.

The cookie☙ or the cake make ☐ me feel better.

A glass of milk or a hug also help ☐!

The Fabulous Forest of WOW

Deep in the forest of WOW, Owl was hunting for something. He looked high up in the leaves of tall trees.

He searched among the bushes.

He scratched at the long grass to see if he could find them.

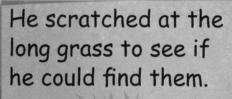

Suddenly, Owl sees Magpie sitting on a branch.

What are you looking for, Owl? Perhaps I can help you.

I'm looking for some noun plural endings. And I'm looking for some verb singular endings.

Plurals? I don't think I know what they are.

Owl described them.

a rabbit   two rabbit🐝   three rabbit🐝

hop ~ hop🐝   run ~ run🐝

Rabbit🐝 hop and run.   A rabbit hop🐝 and run🐝.

Magpie helped Owl in his search.

Back at the WOW School, Owl was preparing for his class. Today's topic was on subject-verb agreement.

The SUBJECT and the VERB of a sentence must agree:

1) When the SUBJECT is singular,
the VERB must also be singular.

The **otter** | **swims** in the lake.
SUBJECT   VERB

The SUBJECT and the VERB of a sentence must agree:

2) When the SUBJECT is plural,
the VERB must also be plural.

The **otters** | **swim** in the lake.
SUBJECT   VERB

19

How do you know when a SUBJECT is singular or plural, Owl?

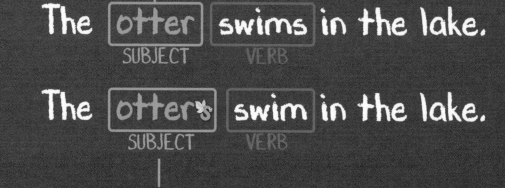

Otter is singular because it refers to one otter, and it has no plural ending.

The [otter] [swims] in the lake.
      SUBJECT   VERB

The [otters] [swim] in the lake.
      SUBJECT   VERB

Otters is plural because it refers to more than one otter, and it has a plural ending **s**.

Do you still remember our lesson on plural nouns?

How do you tell when a VERB is singular or plural, Owl?

Swims is singular. It goes with a singular SUBJECT and it has a singular verb ending s.

The [otter] swims in the lake.
SUBJECT   VERB

The [otters] swim in the lake.
SUBJECT   VERB

Swim is plural. It goes with a plural SUBJECT and so it has no singular verb ending.

We must also learn to spell singular verbs properly, just like we learnt to spell plural nouns.

1. To make the singular present tense, we usually put an -s at the end of the verbs.

    walk → walks   hide → hides   moo → moos

    step → steps   agree → agrees

Except:

2. For verbs that end in -s, -ss, -sh, -ch, -x, add -es.

    pass → passes   reach → reaches   fix → fixes

3. For verbs ending in a consonant and -y, change the y to an i and add -es.

    fly → flies   try → tries   study → studies

4. For verbs ending in a vowel and -y, just add -s.

    pray → prays   enjoy → enjoys   buy → buys

5. For some verbs, there are no regular rules.

    is → are   have → has   do → does   echo → echoes

Let's try and see if you can use the rules to spell these singular verbs.

	Singular Verbs	Plural Verbs	Which rule did you use?
1		miss	
2		smile	
3		grow	
4		do	
5		reply	
6		play	
7		catch	
8		worry	
9		wish	
10		relax	
11		were	
12		stir	

Dear Parents,

In this volume, children are introduced to SUBJECT-VERB agreement. In English, SUBJECTS are very often nouns or rather noun phrases that start a sentence. In Volume 8, we learnt that noun phrases are strings of words in which a noun combines with an article, a quantifier and/or adjectives.

To learn SUBJECT-VERB agreement, it is important to have children notice whether the noun in the noun phrase is singular or plural — they should notice the "s" at the end of the nouns. This helps us decide whether we need to add an "s" to the verb to make it singular.

We also introduced SUBJECT-VERB agreement when a conjunction is used. And makes the SUBJECT plural. Or is a little more complicated and requires children to pay attention to the noun closest to it. In grammar, this is called the proximity rule.

Page	Possible Answers

8-9

The <u>soldiers</u> train hard every day.   My <u>teacher</u> loves to sing.
The <u>soldier</u> trains hard every day.   All my <u>teachers</u> love to sing.

An <u>anteater</u> eats as many as a thousand ants a day.
<u>Anteaters</u> eat as many as a thousand ants a day!

Frogs <u>swim</u> very well.   The lizards <u>climb</u> up the tree.
The little frog <u>hops</u> very quickly.   That lizard <u>looks</u> lost.

These boys love to play football.
The boy usually <u>kicks</u> the ball with his left foot.

15

Either the green cough syrup or the big white pills <u>taste</u>[s] the worst.
My sister or my brothers <u>cheer</u>[ ] me up with lovely treats.
The cookies or the cake <u>make</u>[s] me feel better.
A glass of milk or a hug also <u>help</u>[ ]!

23

	Singular Verbs	Plural Verbs	Which rule did you use?
1	misses	miss	2
2	smiles	smile	1
3	grows	grow	1
4	does	do	5
5	replies	reply	3
6	plays	play	4
7	catches	catch	2
8	worries	worry	3
9	wishes	wish	2
10	relaxes	relax	2
11	was	were	5
12	stirs	stir	1

CERTIFICATE OF ACHIEVEMENT

Volume 19

Awarded to

Name _____

for mastering Volume 19

Date _____

Welcome to the **Wonderful World of Words (WOW)**!

This series of books aims to help children learn English grammar in a fun and meaningful way through stories.

Children will read and discover how the people and animals of WOW learn the importance of grammar, as the adventure unfolds from volume to volume.

What's Inside

Imaginative stories that engage children, and help develop an interest in learning grammar

Adventures that encourage children to learn and understand grammar, and not just memorise rules

Games and activities to reinforce learning and check for understanding

About the Author

Dr Lubna Alsagoff is a language educator who is especially known for her work in improving the teaching of grammar in schools and in teacher education. She was Head of English Language and Literature at the National Institute of Education (NIE), and has published a number of grammar resources used by teachers and students. She has a PhD in Linguistics from Stanford University, USA, and has been teaching and researching English grammar for over 30 years.

Published by Marshall Cavendish Children
An imprint of Marshall Cavendish International

A member of the
Times Publishing Group

Printed in Singapore

visit our website at:
www.marshallcavendish.com

CHILDREN
ISBN 978-981-5009-08-8

9 789815 009088